Building A Sight Vocabulary

With Comprehension

The UG Family

CHRISTINE M. WILLIAMS

Copyright © Christine M. Williams.

All rights reserved. No part of this book may be reproduced in any form or by any electronic or mechanical means, including information storage and retrieval systems, without permission in writing from the publisher, except by reviewers, who may quote brief passages in a review.

ISBN: 978-1-64669-978-0 (Paperback Edition)
ISBN: 978-1-64669-979-7 (Hardcover Edition)
ISBN: 978-1-64669-977-3 (E-book Edition)

Some characters and events in this book are fictitious. Any similarity to real persons, living or dead, is coincidental and not intended by the author.

Book Ordering Information

Phone Number: 347-901-4929 or 347-901-4920
Email: info@globalsummithouse.com
Global Summit House
www.globalsummithouse.com

Printed in the United States of America

Dedication

This series of books are dedicated to my grandchildren, C.J., Xaan, Jaden, Christian, Chase and Jocelynn. If it were not for them, I would not have developed this program.

Contents

Directions for using this book 1

THE UG FAMILY 4

BUG 6

DUG 7

JUG 8

MUG 9

PUG 10

RUG 11

TUG 12

Directions for using this book

Today we will be learning about the UG family of words. All the words we use today will have the letters UG as part of it. All you will have to do is say the letter sound in front of it, than say the word UG. **Have the child say the blended letters UG**. Now what sound does the first letter make? **Have them say the sound.** Now add that sound to the UG, to make the new word. Continue with all the words in the family.

Together with child cut out the words from the back of the book. Say the words as you complete the cutting, and place them on the table. If possible let you child cut the words with safety scissors. Get some paste and paste the words to some cardboard. Than place the words on a door, wall or poster board with the child's help. Hang the list of words at their level. They should be able to point to the word and say it. **Total time for this is 15 minutes.**

Try to review the words at least **twice** a day. **Have them point to the word as he/she says it.** Review those words at least two days before adding the others on the list the third day. Tell them that these words are connecting words to make a sentence.

Do the same things with the new words, **say them, cut them, and hang them.**

Day two: Review words. Say and point to words. Use pictures to discuss the words and its various meanings. **For this age child we do not give parts of speech. The word connects with other words to make you understand what someone is saying.**

Day Three: Review words again. This time play a game you can say the word as I point to it. **DO NOT point to the words in order. Last, middle, second, forth, etc.**

Add new words. **Say them, cut them and hang them.**

Day Four: Review words again. Play how many words do you know. Point to the words in any order and have the child read the words. Do this for five minutes maximum. Make a new set of words using cardboard which is best. Spread these words on the floor in any order. Call out a word and have the child step on the word.

Day Five: Review words again. Place words on the floor again. Have the child find the word. They can step on it, or pick it up. After playing have the child to sit down to read the silly sentences provided. Talk about the sentences! Does this sentence make sense? You and the child can also create your own silly sentences. Do this for five-ten minutes maximum.

Day Six: Review words from previous week and add new words. Put all words on the floor and call out a word to have your child find it. With both sets of words make sentences. Talk about the sentence. Does it make sense? This helps with comprehension.

Try to make at least 10 sentences using all the words. Words can be used in more than one sentence.

As you continue to add new families of words, keep the old word families hanging up so the child can review them on a daily basis. Also don't forget to play the games. This makes learning FUN. You can add a new family of words weekly.

THE UG FAMILY

Bug	Mug

Dug	Pug

Hug	Rug

Jug	Tug

was   this

for

BUG

DUG

JUG

MUG

PUG

RUG

TUG

READ THESE SILLY SENTENCES

The bug dug on the rug.

This jug was the mug.

Tug on the rug for the mug.

Tug the dog and cat.

The fat pug sat on the rug.

The pan with the can ran.

Hug the bug on the mug.

MAKE YOUR OWN SILLY SENTENCES

SEEK AND FIND

Find and Circle the word families in each row. There are some connecting words in the row as well.

A	B	T	H	I	S	C	D	B	U	G
M	U	G	E	F	F	O	R	G	H	I
J	U	G	J	K	L	M	Y	M	N	O
P	Q	R	W	A	S	S	T	D	U	G
U	V	W	P	U	G	X	Y	Z	O	F
A	B	C	H	U	G	D	E	R	U	G
F	G	H	I	J	K	T	U	G	I	S

How many extra letters did you find on each row? Count them.

What did the extra letters make?

ANSWER PAGE

Row 1 There are 4 letters   ab   THIS   cd   BUG

Row 2 There are 5 letters   MUG   ef   FOR   ghi

Row 3 There are 6 letters   JUG   jkl   MY   mno

Row 4 There are 5 letters   pqr   WAS   st   DUG

Row 5 There are 6 letters   Uvw   PUG   xyz   OF

Row 6 There are 5 letters   abc   HUG   de   RUG

Row 7 There are 8 letters   fgh   ijk   TUG   is

The alphabet

Color the picture of the PUG

Color the picture of the bug.

Cut and paste these words on cardboard (Example: cereal box, shoe box, folder or 3X5 cards).

Copy and cut another set of these words.
Cut and hang these words on a wall or door

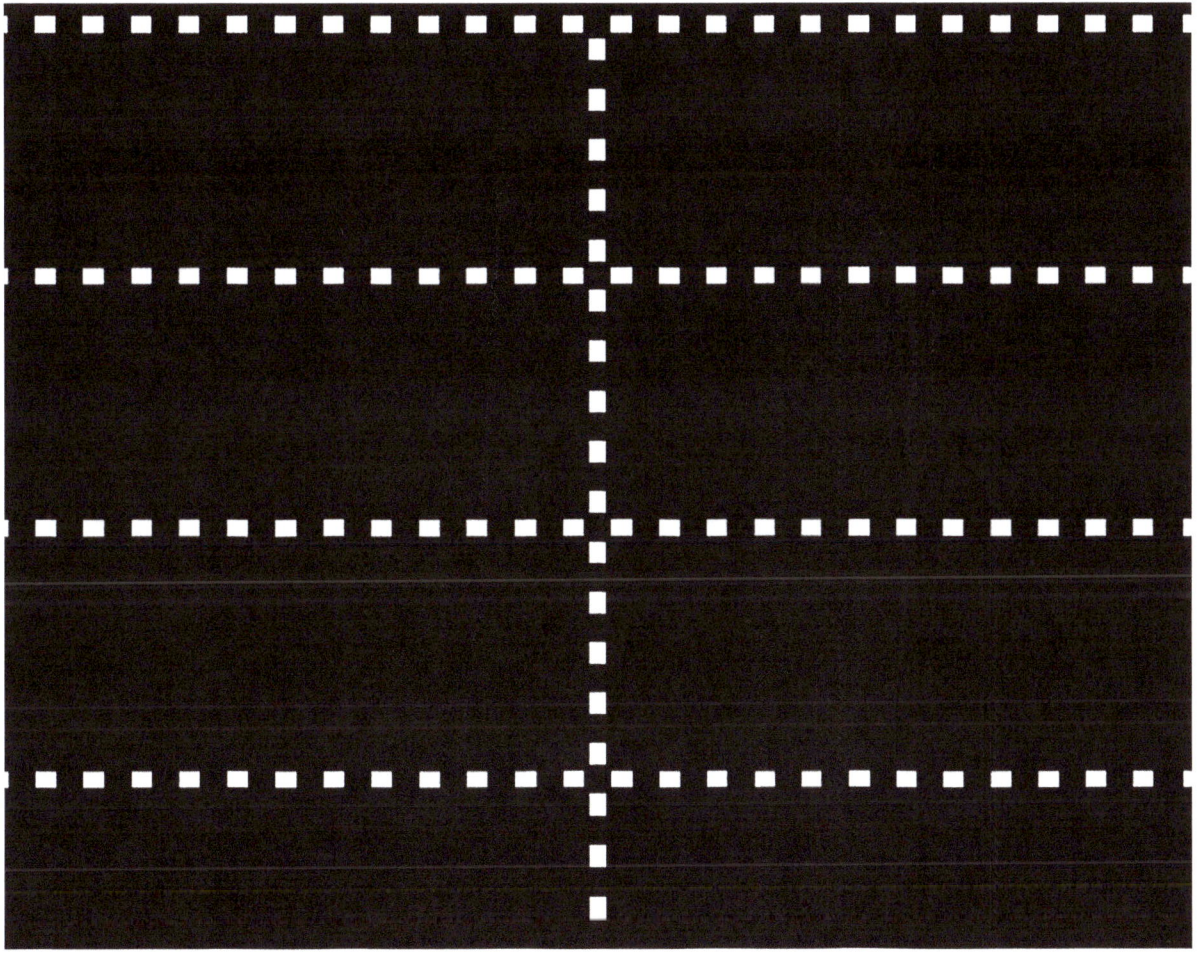

Cut and paste these words on cardboard (Example: Cereal box, shoe box, folder or 3X5 cards).

Copy and cut another set of these words.
Cut and hang these words on a wall or door

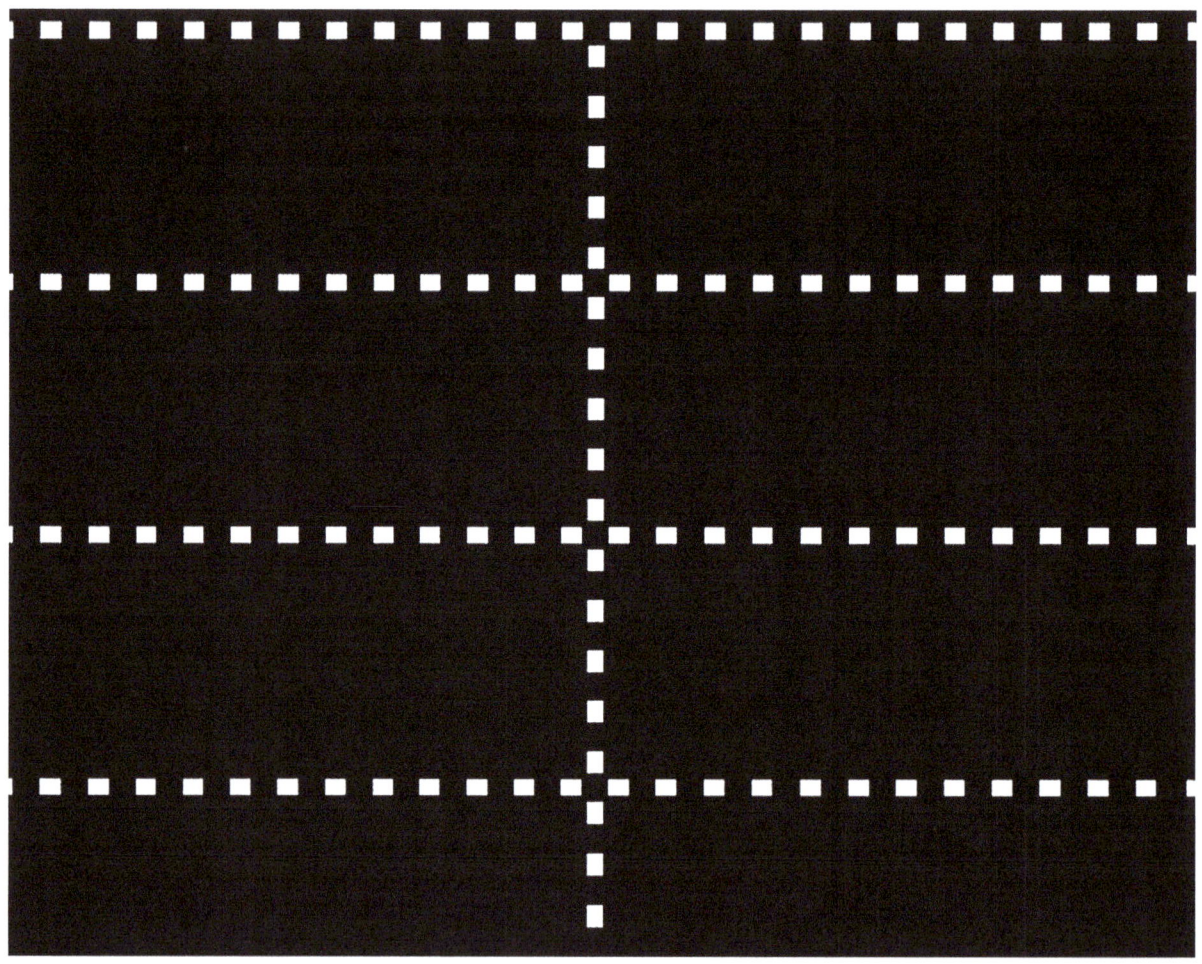

www.ingramcontent.com/pod-product-compliance
Lightning Source LLC
LaVergne TN
LVHW072114060526
838200LV00061B/4885